CW00520226

# Geraldine Green

# Passing Through

**Indigo Dreams Publishing**

First Edition: Passing Through
First published in Great Britain in 2018 by:
Indigo Dreams Publishing
24, Forest Houses
Cookworthy Moor
Halwill
Beaworthy
Devon
EX21 5UU

www.indigodreams.co.uk

Geraldine Green has asserted her right under the Copyright, Designs and Patents Act 1988 to be identified as the author of this work.

© 2018 Geraldine Green

ISBN 978-1-910834-79-4

British Library Cataloguing in Publication Data. A CIP record for this book can be obtained from the British Library.

*This book is sold subject to the condition that it shall not, by way of trade or otherwise, be lent, re-sold, hired out, or otherwise circulated without the author's and publisher's prior consent in any form of binding or cover other than that in which it is published and without a similar condition including this condition being imposed on the subsequent purchaser.*

Designed and typeset in Palatino Linotype by Indigo Dreams. Cover design by Ronnie Goodyer.

Printed and bound in Great Britain by 4edge Ltd.

Papers used by Indigo Dreams are recyclable products made from wood grown in sustainable forests following the guidance of the Forest Stewardship Council.

For my husband Geoff, his support, love and encouragement;
for Uncle Ossy who inspired me;
for my many kind and supportive poet friends
and for Bardsea, beach that cradled me as a baby.

# Acknowledgements

Poems in this collection have appeared in: *Stone Renga*, Tail Feathers Press, Santa Fe, New Mexico, eds. Tom Murphy and Alan Berecka; *Qualia* ed. Roselle Angwin; *My Dear Watson, The Bees Knees*, ed. Rebecca Bilkau; *Curlew Calling* Numenius Press, ed. Karen Lloyd; *The Raspberry and the Rowan*, Cumbria Wildlife Trust; *The City Zine*, ed. Kathy Smith, Ohio, USA; Haiku Calendar 2017 ed. Walter E. Harris III Long Island, USA; *SpeakEasy Magazine*, Vol.1 ed. Nick Pemberton; *Watershed* – an anthology in response to Storm Desmond, eds. Nick Pemberton, Ann Wilson, Geraldine Green; *Long Island Quarterly* USA, ed. George Wallace; *Like Light*, Bright Hill Press 25th anniversary anthology, Catskills USA, ed. Bertha Rogers

## Also by Geraldine Green:

Salt Road
The Other Side of the Bridge
A Wing and a Prayer
Poems of a Mole Catcher's Daughter
Passio
The Skin

# Foreword

*Passing through* is a collection of poems, prose poems and poetic prose. Taken together they form a love letter to Cumbria, in childhood and through into later adulthood. Mainly based in the south and west of the county, some venture farther afield. They are also, in part, a celebration of my year as writer-in-residence Brantwood, Coniston.

Written from 2013 onwards, they swoop and dive back and forth as walking daily along familiar paths and tracks shakes this writer's memory.

Geraldine Green

# CONTENTS

# Passing Through

*When despair for the world grows in me*
*and I wake in the night at the least sound*
*in fear of what my life and my children's lives may be,*
*I go and lie down where the wood drake*
*rests in his beauty on the water, and the great heron feeds.*
*I come into the peace of wild things*

– Wendell Berry, *The Peace of Wild Things*

**Listen**

I am listening to my age.
It is humming of fear and fascination.
The bees inside my head sting me into waking.

I want to take these 60 bees –
Wild and unswarmed – place them
in the lift.

       The lift will take them down
to the basement.

      I hear them,
           the bees.
They are angry inside their coffin of steel.

*Shhh.* Their humming diminishes

all I can hear is my breathing

it is coming from behind
      the ochre door.
The ochre door that sounds like spices
      and Christmas.

One door is painted yellow
        It sounds like madness.
I place my palm against its madness
    lean closer,
           Listen.

The bees are back; swollen with pollen.

Their brownblack furred  back legs
      articulate their fury.

If I hold my breath
         they may not hear.
If I take off my shoes
               slip them
inside my pocket
                tiptoe along
         this hall to another door
I may find myself looking.

Perhaps this door,
         door of cool cerulean blue,
                    may heal me.

## Stone Renga

What do I know of stones?
Flat, mud-grey ones

on Foulney Island. Layer upon layer
heaped up for feet to scramble and slide on.

What do I know of stones?
Those at Aldingham, dark grey

round as a bird's egg
shot through with milky quartz

in circles and crosses that lie
warm and smooth in my palm.

What do I know of stones?
Limestone dragons on Birkrigg

dinosaur-shapes glint white
fissures on ancient pavements.

What do I know of stones, their secret
of fossils: ammonites, ferns, feathers

spiralled, whorled worlds imprinted within them
ready  to take flight

when their old stone-bodies
crack open.

## Lark, Lorelei of air and sky

Now it is cool on Birkrigg Common, the Isle of Man clear in the distance under thin blue sky, while Black Combe's bulk is cotton-woolled in kettle-steam cloud. I think of John Clare and enclosures, he'd have loved the wide open space of this common land where larks sing "above below behind beyond", where limestone rocks lie like sleeping dinosaurs, some blocks mark a path – larks, like Lorelei, want to lure a walker away from nests and young with song – larks, lovers of wide open space and freedom.

Why Tudors & Elizabethans ate larks' tongues in aspic is beyond me, such tiny things. Did they believe that eating them would put them in good voice to sing matins and psalms, Capella, luminous and clear as the star of that name?

Birkrigg appears higher today, whether it's the clouds low down in the middle ground on the fells, I don't know, but Bardsea village and spire seem way below, to the south and east as I swing round on the homeward path, checking for ash die-back as I go.

# I am no longer myself on these sands

*"I am no longer myself but part of a life beyond myself"*
    – Nan Shepherd *'The Living Mountain'*

I walk, feet spread, mud filled, across these sands.
I walk in whatever weather
the flow of tides and turn of moon remain the same
I walk, listen to curlews in season

listen to peewits their call of reason unknown to me,
their tumble and dive, their black and white
oval shaped wings that flip over and over these sands
as I stop and stand in amazement.
Listen. To their *pee-wit!* their *pee-wit!*
Lap-winged sham of lame wing
protects their young.

I am no longer myself in these sands.

My feet take on the shape of flecked webbed feathers
of cockles ribbed and broken hashed and unstirred.
I am no longer myself on these mudflats.
I am the over and under of goldfinches, caught
in the startle of their carouselled calling
woven into reeds tasselled mauve and silver.
I am slashed flesh cockle ribbed
toe scrabbled sea bed.
I am a nine holed flute rooted in mud.

I am sea asters in summer.
I am white honeyed blossom.
I am bee strewn fingers across marram-grassed ways.

I am the plovers' tumble
I am frosted teasels.

I am no longer who I am but another
who nose dives towards the ripple of water
I am the swallow-scythed air of summer.
I am the crabs who come inshore on a full moon
floating and new, crushed by silver light
whose whiteness flecks this mud's black-slicked body.
I am the eider ducks' astonished *awww*.

I am mudflats. I am home.

## Always the flight

The song of freedom hangs in the air above skylarks and bracken. Migrating curlews pass through, land briefly to overwinter from moorland to coast and back again. Always movement of quicksilvered sand and changing seasons

shapeshifting from black to white, red to brown to yellow to August, September to April. Always the movement of gulls: swift acting, nose diving. Always the pattern of possibilities, changing shape and skin. Autumn to winter, spring to summer and back again.

Shrill call of terns defending their territory. Flying of red kites over fell and estuary. Puncturing of clouds, thundering tides, movement of birds and humans. Red to white, black and gold, silver and red, tawny skinned, wrinkled, smooth. Flesh of old. Flesh of young. Bright and dying.

## A little bit of bread

There's a hen blackbird drinking from the bird-bath. In fact I watch her almost daily as I stand at the kitchen window washing up. She flies in over the hawthorn, sits on the rim of the bath, amid squabbles of sparrows in the beech hedge, looks around, then delicately takes a sip, head back, the water trickling down her tipped back throat. Again. And again.

Throat full, head back, belly full of eggs – she drinks with grace, unlike the magpies, who bend sharply, chunkily, swaggeringly and drink, almost grabbing at the water. Once, twice, quick look around. And off!

Buds are coming through on the hawthorns. I never really looked closely at them before. How rose pink and shiny they are, how, from that deep pink tight bud springs the fresh green 'bread and cheese' we ate as children.

How the yellowhammer sings it to us 'a little bit of bread and no cheese!'

## Juniper, Crag Head

I'd like to sleep beneath this ancient Juniper, twisted as it is, bent low by prevailing westerlies blown in from the Irish Sea. Bivvy for one night only, or perhaps more, if I were brave enough. If I were underneath this old tree's sanctuary, this evergreen that cattle have trodden round, keeper of flame, this incense tree, maker of gin and dreams and love that has seen many winters.

I'd like to sleep below its twisted arms, wake to see morning gold or fog ridden. Wake to look across and see the Old Man of Coniston. To wake, after sleep beneath this ancient Juniper, twisted as it is, breathe in its incense.

## Mining, Coniston

What I know about Copper.

That its element is *Cu,*
when oxidised it goes greenblue.

That my Grandmother used to have a kettle
made from this metal, it stood on the hearth
in her cottage below Coppermines Valley

its handle worn smooth. I know that her hands
were gnarled and boled like tree roots
veins raised like greenblue streams

on the river bed of a map that shone copper
when the sun struck her wafered skin.

Know that when you swim in the tarn below
Dow Crag and you open your eyes underwater
you enter the milk blue world of Cyprium

become – if only for a moment
                        – the element of Cyprus.

## Pond near Lake Bank

Crouched
on the edge
of the pond
feet pressed
on sphagnum moss
the toads I watch
gaze back at me
already alerted
to my coming
by heavy treads
felt yards away

I gaze into water.

Small, black translucent balls of light
threaded onto invisible filaments float out on strings
below the pond's dark surface.

## Coniston

Lake speaks
      twigs of boned ash
ruffle the wind

## Nacreous Sky

Mother-of-pearl in the west –
     who'd have thought so shell like
a sky after this storm?

## Lake Bank, Coniston Water

Sometimes, as I did this afternoon
after my morning class,
sometimes I just need to sit
and listen
to the sounds of water
doing nothing in particular
just being
its normal watery self
in a beck, tumbling
from the fell
or in the sound of mallards
their *quawwk* of calling
their ripples
their *vee* formation
their fooling me into thinking
I'd seen a pike
rising.

Sometimes, just
to sit and listen
in this place of calm water
sometimes in its squall
of storms
but today, today
in its tranquility
of mirrors.

# Siblings

*After Joe Brainard*

I remember the first time I went to Kendal, *how far is it?*
I asked, *25 miles there and 25 miles back.* 50 miles. I wanted
to travel further.

I remember Kendal Mint Cake and K shoes. I remember
my sister flooded out of her flat when the Kent overtopped
its bank one winter.

I remember the first time I went to Appleby Horse Fair
paddled among Piebalds and Skewbalds in the River Eden
savouring the words: *pie bald, skew bald.*

I don't remember that the coat of arms for Westmorland
is two red bars, a golden apple tree (for Appleby) a ram's head
and a shearsman hook.

I do remember that the Helm Wind is the only named wind
in Britain, blows in on north easterlies over Cross Fell, is called
Helm, wears a helmet of clouds, is fierce and blows for days.

I remember seeing tatty plastic bags tangled in branches along
the River Lune just below the Radical Steps, Kirkby Lonsdale.

I remember being amazed at the audacity of a man, a stranger,
who climbed a rock on Firbank Fell, gazed down onto a chapel
beneath him, listened to the preacher in the *steeple-house* below.

I remember Westmorland, sibling to the Furness Peninsula,
was once called Lancashire North of the Sands.

Sibling too, to Cumberland the wild, dark country beyond
Black Combe.

## Whaup

*"I take my gladness in the… sound of the curlew instead of the*
*laughter of men"*
        – 'The Seafarer' Anon. Anglo-Saxon poet

In the absence of curlew I must attempt
to call it down, to call it back to fell and shore
call it back to sing the moor alive once more.

In the absence of curlew clouds must learn
to bring back spring, to lay cloud eggs on upland soil
to curve cloud bodies into curlew-grace

into speckled feathers that mimic mica-sand and
mottled stones, the guarding of eggs, slow beating
of wing, curved-down bill that probes the earth

for worms, the shore for crabs, its long wail
the cry of the dead waiting to be re-born.
I must again recall the great whaup's warning

the dead's return from dreaming. Listen
to what the night is saying through the piercing
cry of *cur leee,* of *cur-lee.*

## Moth, Eycott Hill

Today I held a moth on my hand.
No, a moth held me
a place to rest for an instant.
Today held me.
Captured among bog asphodel
germander speedwell and poets.

Among rowan splitting rock, wild raspberry
among shifting wind and skies
the place before and behind us
among volcanics and eyebright
I was held in a nest
of shifting belonging.
In a web of sphagnum
and rough hawkbit
in a cry of curlews above

a round sheepfold, held
and caught
to be fastened to the world again
on a pin of spider grass,
to be held intact like rockfastlichen
in the curvetting of ravens,
their *crawwking* cries
in the language of flowers
horned message on red clover,
green striped white petals
on Grass of Parnassus,
in the feeling of being held again and again
in an embrace so wide it hurt.

Today a moth held me.
Its embrace of clover,
embrace of wild silver,

embrace of sunlight
spearing our eyes
with lichen, echoing of meadows.

A baby's rattle, yellow and frail, shook its fist at me.
I replied with no talk.
All I asked for was given

in the listening of raven.
In the cry of curlew,
in the weaving of one colour into another
purple into mauve into pink into yellow
into white into greens and mosses
into fog of Yorkshire grasses
plaited skies and voices of people
into the meadow that grew from our fingertips
into each of our molecules into rasps and snorts,
dark skies and the splendour of unknown moons.

Today a moth split me open.

Its soft dust on my right fleshed hand
just below my forefinger between it and my thumb.
It stayed there, the moth, bright and settled
before flying off, its underwing orange.

## Samhain: A Door

Oak, Eycott, Hag and Hecate, Aiket and Druid, Reflector of Names, Old Golden Bough, Apple of Samhain, Old Woman of Knowledge, Oak, Eycott, Aiket, Dryad, Oak Apple

Blossom of Youth, Keeper of Secrets, Aiket Gate, Eycott Hill, Bough of the Golden, Oak Apple Dew, Dryad and Aiket, Eycott, Druid, Holder of Secrets, Golden Bough, Old Woman, Oak Appled Blossom

Hidden in Folds of Fellsides and Coppice, Oak Apple, Golden Cheeked, Maiden of Apple, Bringer of Knowledge, Oak Appled Spinner, Hidden in Spider, Insect Weaver, Woven of Mysteries, Eycott, Aiket, Oak and Druid, Dwr

Weint Watter, Weaver of Lakes, Winder of Sapping, Makar of Steel, Dwr and Duir, Drear and Dryad, Aiketgate, Eycott, Oak Leaved Watter, Oak Twigs for Fuel, Acorns for Fodder, Split Oppen the Acorn, Door to the Future.

## Companions

Drove back from a visit to a friend's last week, along a narrow, single-track road in north Cumbria. The day had been one of those days, weather-wise, that makes you simultaneously want to hunker down inside, or go outside, fling your arms wide and say 'blow wind, crack your cheeks!' – Lear-like.

Well, I did both. Ate soup and soaked up conversation with my friends, spoke of the joy that age can bring of seeing things almost afresh, so that even the simple act of feeding birds brings a quiet content.

Shared an anecdote of a red squirrel's antics in deep snow we had back in March. How it tried to climb the bird-table pole, kept slipping, chittered to itself fell off into soft, piled-up snow. You could see the frustration and humph! in that red squirrel's face, a clear expression of disgust in its scrunched-up nose.

When I walked Roy after lunch, I met a couple of walkers who had set off along the Cumbrian-way, which starts in the Gill, Ulverston. They told me "We didn't bother going over Skidda' as the wind was bad enough on top of High Pike."

One of them pointed to Roy, a Border Collie, and said, "We saw a shepherd with a few of those up on the tops, just think. All the miles those dogs run, gathering up the sheep in all weathers!" We looked at Roy, eager in the rain and high wind to get going again, down the lane.

The 'lane', it's a clarty old farm track, but the views over to the west, north and of the steep road climbing out of the village, soon to be lined with yolk-coloured gorse, is one engraved in the eyes of my heart.

It's a track of the badgers that inhabit this fellside. I've seen them late at night when walking a variety of dogs. Seen them stop and pause at the corner by the beech tree. Seen them, black and silver creatures of shadow and moon.

## Today

Light on catkins,
sulphur-yellow against
the blue of sky

unselfconscious cries
of oyster catchers,
dunlins and terns

I sit at the laneside,
between Bardsea
and Birkrigg,

my back against
the sun-warmed wall
look across the bay

to silver-blue sands
that turn to caramel
when the tide goes out.

Hear hedgerow birds:
blue tits, sparrows,
a robin and the *chit*

*chack* scold of wren
as it dodges and hides
in  the limestone wall.

*Troglodyte troglodyte,*
so small a cave-dweller
– so loud a voice.

## A playfulness of otters

Couple of things I learned yesterday: that freshwater mussels now live in Ulverston canal; that otters play with stones. The man who told me also shared the fact that one evening, his head torch on, he walked down the canal and saw an otter playing and sliding on the ice.

Saw two swans today pulling and hoiking dried bullrush leaves, reeds, stems green and knotted. A green nested platform created for new life.

Now the female is nesting... head tucked under her wing... white against green.

Other swan pairs are also joining in, pulling, hoiking.

This love of life, its urgency, in the green light of spring, bewildering when you stop and look.

**Seeing**
*Professor's Garden, Brantwood*

When I look up I see what might be a wren's nest, tucked in between the second and third beam. It's made of moss and grass, pieces of mortar cling to it; horse hair too, black and coarse from the old way of making wattle and daub. Last year's nest, I guess.

How many eggs were laid here, just in front of me, and above as I look up? A snail trail, few inches to my left, graceful slime of silver; noticing one I see more.

I wonder: what was the name of the horse?

## Fog gave the woods silence

What sounds there were – sea birds in the distance,
woodpecker, song thrush – echoed round the trees.

I found a place of violets. Fragile, purple, bright green.

Mist heightened the colours of leaves: miniature lady's mantle,
wild garlic. No white starred flowers yet.

## Who knows what I might see today

a weasel, like the one that sat opposite me yesterday?

Miniature meerkat that sat up still and straight, bobbed up,
in fact, watched me with bright boot-button eyes – I

didn't move – hardly breathed – it turned
looked at my dog, panting among wild garlic
then darted into bramble.

Nothing. No sign. Slight rustle, a little closer. Then.
Up it popped again.
We sat like that for a while.

Me, the dog and weasel.

I had time to admire its cream-lemon bib,
its small paws, its uprightness.

Movement near the beach gate startled us.

### Above my head in the Dogrose
*Near Eskdale Green*

is a wren, chit chattering. Scolding us for being so close to her
nest beneath the garage eaves.

On the third day she became used to our presence, sat on the
branch of a slender ash tree branch and chittered.

Silhouetted against the morning sun her tail cocked and flickering
her small body alight and alive in amber light.

Each note fine-tuned and aimed at us. Intruders
near her dwelling.

### Dead cattle hides

piled high, curled and dried, autumn leaves driven from the yard on flat bed lorries. Hides tanned with oak bark tannin, stinking air down

West End Lane. A child rides her bike through flooded lanes, legs askew, handlebars dripping honeysuckle, dog roses and meadow sweet

antidote to stench of dead cattle hides piled high, curled and dried, dead leaves on flat bed lorries. Flash of turquoise by Tanyard bridge –

kingfisher arrows downriver.

## Pristine

Muffled *bhoooooooom* in the distance
like someone blowing on paper wrapped
around a comb, sound of traffic fades
along the Coast Road.

Here, on a bench dappled with shadows
of ramson leaf, above, shapeshifting clouds
at my feet a bee couples with wild garlic

its yellowbrown body furrows
into whitestarred flowers, it sips
green nectar.

Nearby cuckoo pint, lords and ladies,
adam and eve, hooded cobras; cloaks
wrapped around the dark brown phallused
ring of male hairs – insect trap for the unwary

Recall the jackdaw I saw last week
on the iron-ored path, pristine
in death, its silvery sheen, pale eyes gleaming.

## Piel Island swimming

Swam in moonlight
in the silence of waves
in the moan of seals
in the hisshush of sea
off the jetty at Piel.

## Giving voice

how to give a voice in anothers voice?
a wolf voice a coyote voice a river voice
a hedgehog voice. how to give a song
to the coyote song the red wolf song
the curlew song. how to give a voice ◉
to the river song the mountain song ◉
the earth song the you song the me ◉
song the without the earth voice of◉
coyote song wolf song hedgehog ◉
song without the mountain
song ◉the wild mountain
thyme song sand
dune song, song
the seal song
the toads◉
song
the you◉
song the me◉
song without them, then,◉
who are we?

## Grey seal

Your eyes meet mine.
Your curiosity also mine.
Your bathing in the sea
as we do as kids and with kids
and dogs, splashing.

Your home is the ocean.
You're dependent on fish, crustaceans,
the constant currents of motion.

Shared life sprung
from mud and salt water
only
we have the power
to pull the trigger.

**Ghost Stones Bay**

Cormorants
        at the tide's edge,
wings outspread.
        Dark angels of the sea.

**Watching**

the bull seal swim
    neck curved
        around its mate, eager
            as a hungry teenager

        watched them
    their playfulness
their language of sea.

**That moment of hare**

The one I saw this afternoon
as I drove along the back lanes
between Scales and Aldingham.

The one that darted out
from the hedge-topped stone-walled field,
paused mid flight, then stopped.

Bright fur an amalgam of sunlight and spring
alongside cold metal.
Antennae'd ears turned towards me.

I drove slowly away.

## I recall our walk in Burns Beck Moss

the softness of ground, the softness of feet, the hush of bodies, the quiet chat and the moss cushioning us, our feet, our chat, our bodies, our thoughts, the frogs' stretched balletic legs, their crouched sanctuary among the sphagnum, speeding away from boots and trainers, our feet on cushioned silence, crushing their territory.

**Seen from Brown Pike**

two butterflies
        sail
                into space
                                over jagged crags
below us

                we hold our breath
                        they
                                launch
                                        into air

## Light, Grizedale Forest

Today I became snagged on light. Not only light, the way it reflects on water and leaves – these leaves, I mean, on the bridge, snagged on light, like me, like stone, cold, unsobered, alive with spitting, splitting, alight with leaves, wet leaves, the one in the centre of this bridge here, leaves alive, bristled and veined, coppered and alight, on a stone cold sobering bridge, somewhere in a forest, today maybe, maybe Grizedale.

## Quiet Devoke Water

We walked amid silence and skylarks. Among bog asphodel and miniature forests of round-leaf sundew, bright orange and open to insects – their delicate feathered 'jaws' awake and receptive. As we were to the silence. To the quiet, companionable chat of tiny rills bubbling up behind us, as they spilled down the fells. Up and out and over, down to the water. To Devoke.

To get there drive up from Ulpha Bridge from the south, or the George Fourth pub Eskdale, from the northwest.

Park up. Walk along the track and head west, from the rusted-iron signpost signalling 'Eskdale and Whitehaven', signalling 'Broughton' and east to 'Stanley Ghyll'.

We plodged through a couple of fozzy bogs, wrapped up as we were yet peeling off a layer or two as the south westerly wind was warm, then a sudden plunge into cloud caused a slight chill on our skin. Looked west, imagined the Irish Sea stared at by Sellafield and who knows? Soon maybe giant pylons will march from Moorside to Rampside, watched over by the Iron, or Bronze, Age settlement.

Canada geese sailed southwards towards us from the tiny island in the west and south of the water. An island of bent pines, juniper and isolation.

Yet its presence made us feel at home as we sat and drank our tea. At home in this remote upland area. At home in the company of pink granite, in the peace of air and wind and water sundew and bracken

Herdwicks and larks, bog asphodel and tormentil. We were at home among the crags and fissures, at home by the steelgrey windruffled water, in the smell of sheep, the invisible sea.

Turning east we made our way back to the car, parked by the rusted iron signpost.

## Fishing on the outgoing tide

Opposite,
Heysham power station,
to the west, across the Irish Sea,
offshore wind farms.
Inland, Centrica BAE and
among all this
grey seals,
cormorants,
pink-footed geese,
curlews, dunlins –

a kestrel I startled,
as it startled me
sat on the roof
of the Groyne Hide
close by to where I
perched on a plank bench
watched seals fishing
in the outgoing tide.

Swing your gaze around:
Ingleborough, Piel Island,
Black Combe, Scafells
Coniston Old Man
Dow Crag, Red Screes,
Kidsty Pike, Froswick,
Ill Bell, the Howgills,

dizzying mantra, audience
to the winged-tide,
dazzling your eyes

A seal, sleek-nosed,
wave-shined, mimics
sun-splattered sea.

# I could wrap

this moment up
each shell and turn
of the tide
each swell, bob and snort
of the seal
each tiny robotic movement
each daft dance of us all
snail, shell, ant, moth, or
spider in the bath
each crab-appled tree
each nook-crannied dream

I could parcel it into a symphony
Bach perhaps, or maybe Verdi –
some kind of green orchestral calling
of blackbirds, crows, rooks and starlings,
small, black silhouettes perched
on telephone wires

wood pigeons, their precarious
balancing on copper beeches
their snatching of beech nuts
their knowledge of winter.

## Steadfast

*And all manner of thing shall be well* – Julian of Norwich

sometimes, when you listen to a hedgehog feed
the world steadies itself on its axis and you feel ok.
sometimes when you hear a woodpecker,
deft clatter of beak against solid wood,
the world steadies itself and all is ok.
sometimes, when you recall the softness
of a lapwing chick you held in your hand
as a child you feel a rush of something
other than your self and you feel yes,
ok the world is good
can be good sometime
and sometimes, when the oak
you know so well
that stands just there on your horizon
steadies itself into a ship's mast,
you can feel steady inside somewhere,
feel some kind of steady-ness
that is fed by the lapwing chick
its feathered heartbeat
you held in your childhood palms
and all is well with the world.
all can be well, all is well.

**Passing through**

The monks of Byland Abbey knew
       a thing or two about flood defences
*Thacka   Poaka   Dragley beck*

They built a bund to catch the river
       let it out through culverts, slowly
*Eden   Eamont   Greta   Cocker*

Build a bund to manage water
       *Derwent   Lune*
*Crake*   and *Bela*

*Liza* wanders braided wilded
       'forms banks of stones
and woody debris'

*Smithy   Stanah   Whelpo*
       *Whitecombe*
*Thacka   Poaka   Dragley beck.*

## Poem written on a track near the Howgills

*The earth is a living thing*
        Lucille Clifton

The earth is a living thing
is a cinnabar moth on eyebright
bog asphodel turned
burnt orange on a cloudraced fellside
above a track of poets, eyes
this way and that.
The earth lives inside itself
inside each one of us
*quick now, here, now, always,* wrapped
in the radiator sun. The earth
is a keeper of secrets of bees and pollen
in the vigil of moonrise
in the witness of planets
in the tremor of a mouse as it lies dying
in the talons of hawk.
The earth is an adventure of thistledown
heavy flight of waspwarped drunkenness
a delight of apples, crepe-ing of hoar frost
a greening of spring, closing of a day's eye
the earth is alive
as you are
as I.

## At home on the Bay

Its light, its silver, its mud-tanged-tangle-tongued
salt-licked presence and the birds, dunlins, perhaps,
or knot?

Too far out for us to catch what they were
without binocs. How they swoop and mimic
the murmurations of starlings, but

are not, these wide-winged verses of song
these wing-spread low-tide flit-flight light-tilted
blown along froth

of feather-mimicked pebbles and foam
interpretations of mud and sky
these birds that rise and fall with the incoming tide

this late afternoon beneath the crescent moon
that rises above shavings of licked-clean shells
and bones.

## Lost count

… of the number of lapwings this morning as the high tide came in at Earnse Bay… their high sweet call of *pee wit! pee wit!* merged into the wild white horses as the Irish Sea was at its full, a 9.9 metre tide… full with the sound of oyster catchers, and the white brown flish flash of knot as they turned and burned the water and sky in their silent poem of ballet…

… in the field five horses chomped steadily as a small flock of starlings twittered about them. We walked on nearly to the end of the sand dunes, but stopped. Sat, recalled summer and Walney geraniums in bloom, recalled sea holly, thyme and sea cabbages, recalled other times in the dunes… looked north towards Black Combe, cormorants flew low, pterodactyl-like over the reluctant outgoing tide…

## Untitled

How can I spend tonight inside
when stars and air – so cold –
call me to vigil with them?

**Can you tell me the full moon names?**

Wolf moon, Snow moon, Worm and Pink.
And can you tell me again
the names of the moon at its full?
Pink, Flower, Strawberry and Buck
and when is the Sturgeon, Harvest
and Hunter? August, September
October when fields have been reaped
and harvest is over.

November, the Beaver
before swamps freeze land and water,
frosty and cold before December
when long nights set in,
this moon before Yule
and always an extra moon
is needed.

The blue moon,
the fourth moon.

My moon is red-grained and Green Corn.
Yours is the Worm moon when ice is melting
and the cawing of crows calls spring to its table
when time is ripe for tapping the maple.

But out of the blue
light will soon lengthen,
when Wolf moon is howling

# I found myself in the Blue Room

*In response to an exhibition of photographs of Glen Fender
Meadow by John Ford, in the Blue Room, Brantwood*

I found myself
            in the Blue Room
stunned
            among bilberry

in my perfect overcoat
            of field gentian
                        or perhaps
            grass of Parnassus.

Truth found me
            speechless
                        one more creature
            in this *campestris*
shoulder to shoulder
            with
melancholy thistle
            bog asphodel

I am among mixed flowers.
I am downy birch.
I am butterwort.

Globe flowers light my way
            in dark corners.

Mountain everlasting.
Mountain pansy.

Primula leaves
            are my green-veined
                        tapestry.

*There are many trees*
        *in the meadow*
*the presence of snow*
        *on the distant hills shows*
*how slow a process*
                *is the demise of winter.*

Spring flush of trees, now
        winter is over.
Thaw-filled ponds
        frogs soon will be spawning
in the long-dreamed grasses
        near Glen Fender Meadow.

## NOTES

**P.14**  **Lark, Lorelei of earth and sky:** words in inverted commas are a slight misquote from John Donne's poem *To His Mistress Going to Bed.*

**P.26**  **Whaup:** whaup is a Scottish name for curlew.

**P.55**  **Poem written on a track near the Howgills:** quote italicised mid-poem from *Little Gidding V, Four Quartets* by T S Eliot.

**P.60**  **I found myself in the Blue Room:** *campestris* – of the fields.

*Life's wonderful, lass. Never forget that. Life's wonderful.*

R.I.P. Ossy Coyles
25th August 1919 – 10th December 2016

Indigo Dreams Publishing Ltd
24, Forest Houses
Cookworthy Moor
Halwill
Beaworthy
Devon
EX21 5UU
www.indigodreams.co.uk